The Word of God

Elementary Book 3

by N. A. Woychuk, M. A., Th. D.

Cover and all Illustrations
by Jeffery Scott Terpstra

©NKJV Revised Edition 2000 by N. A, Woychuk.
All rights reserved.
Illustrations ©2000 by Jeffery Terpstra.

Scripture Memory Fellowship
International
P.O. Box 411551 • St. Louis, Missouri 63141

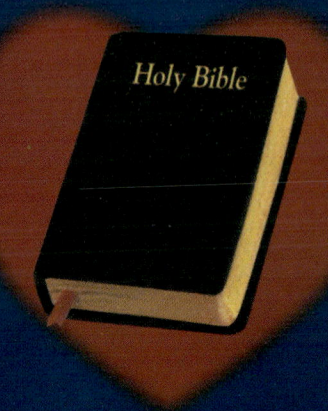

The Bible that is gathering dust,
A weapon that is showing rust
Will not suffice to keep us pure,
Temptation's power to endure
If we would make the foe depart,
God's word must be within the heart.
By these words alone the foe is smitten,
In this our hope: "It is written."

—Tom Welsch, New Jersey
who began memorizing
when in grade school.

Assignment   **Page**

1. God's Word Comes From God 11
2. God's Word Speaks For God 13
3. God's Word Is Pure 15
4. God's Word Is Sure 17
5. His Word Gives Me Light 19
6. His Word Keeps Me Right 21
7. His Word Is My Delight .23
8. His Word Is My Defense 25
9. It Is the Seed of God 27
10. It Is the Strength of Prayer 29
11. It Is the Source of Faith 31
12. It Is the Secret of Life .33
Guide For Parents And Shepherds 4
Rules To Guide The Memorizer 6
The Use of Rewards 7
The Fruit of Memorizing Scripture 8
What is the Bible Like 34
Holy Bible, Book Divine 38
To My Pocket-Bible 39
Scripture Index 40

Guide For Parents And Shepherds

1. Let the memorizers be impressed with the challenge of Scripture memorization. They are enrolled in the course wherein children, young folk and adults throughout the world are participating. They are doing a very big thing, a very serious thing, and one that requires real effort. Let them be thrilled with the sense of accomplishment.

2. Read the whole assignment with the child carefully, including heading, references, and the explanations on the left page. Point out the significance of the art work so that a connection is formed with the assignment heading and the Scriptures.

3. The Scriptures in this Memory Book are printed in the New King James Version. We have other books where the verses are printed in the King James Version. These are available to those who desire them. The art work is not the same.

4. Do not allow mistakes. Be sympathetic and loving, but be fair and firm. Maintain a high standard. Point out the smallest mistakes immediately, and soon he will learn that total accuracy is expected. If the child tries to say a verse and almost succeeds, he should be encouraged, but should be required to do perfect work. Children may try to get by with less.

5. Frequent repetition and continual review are the secret of retaining. Just keep at it in short periods at all times. All through the day and at bedtime, opportunities should be utilized to get at the verses in an enjoyable way.

6. Use every opportunity to relate the meaning of the Scriptures to real life in the experiences of the child, in the home and in the community. Try to establish a connection between the verses and the child's daily life.

7. Hiding God's Word in the heart opens up a new world for meaningful discipline in the home: "Children, obey your parents in the Lord: for this is right' " (Eph. 6: 1).

*Precious promise God has given
to the little passer-by
on the way from earth to heaven,
"I will guide thee with Mine eye."*

*I will guide, I will guide,
"I will guide thee with Mine eye";
on the way from earth to heaven,
"I will guide thee with Mine eye."*

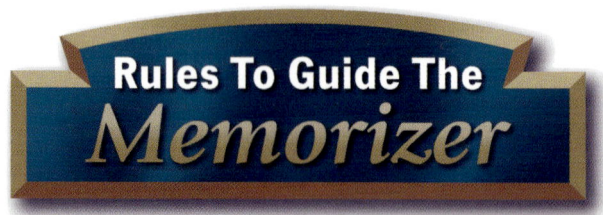

Rules To Guide The Memorizer

1. Memorize the verses exactly as they are printed. Do not add, do not change, and do not leave out any words.

2. In memorizing and reciting give the heading, then the reference, followed by the verse under it.

3. Of course, you *do not* memorize the poems, stories, explanations, etc.

4. You are *not* allowed to recite just part of an assignment. You must recite an entire assignment at one time. Memorize assignments in the order given.

5. You are permitted to recite more than one assignment on the first recitation day, but after that, you may recite only one assignment a week, as you are required to spend the *whole week* preparing each assignment.

6. You must memorize well. You should never have to be prompted. It is a poor recitation if you have to be prompted more than 4 times, and for such a recitation you get a check.

7. By "prompting" we mean drawing attention to a mistake and helping you to recollect and to get the connection in the verses. A word may be suggested, but when you have to be told a phrase or sentence, it is obvious that you are not prepared. Failing to know one assignment may disqualify you. The decision is made by the local Shepherd.

8. You are to recite each week at the set day and hour.

9. If you fail to report to your Shepherd or Hearer one time, you must explain or be disqualified. In case of sickness or unavoidable situations, you may make other arrangements agreeable with your local Shepherd or Hearer.

The Use of Rewards

There are some folks who have an aversion to the idea of rewards for memorizing Scripture. They feel that the thought of rewards corrupts the child's motives. I wonder if they would feel equally strong that the idea of a salary for a pastor might undermine his singleness of heart in preaching the Word, and that it should be withdrawn?

Still, there is a caution to be observed along this line, and we should keep before the children the thought that the Scripture itself is their greatest reward. Furthermore, the rewards we issue are Christian books and camps, which are in themselves a spiritual ministry, and are intended to supplement and extend the profits gained from the Scriptures. We have found through the years that these rewards not only stimulate greater diligence in the work, but they have been a most farreaching spiritual benefit, and have served only to emphasize the value of the Word and not to distract from it. The objections are only academic, and do not merit serious attention.

Little children, like many older ones, do not recognize the value of the Scriptures. It will be up to mother Eunice and grandmother Lois to arrange, to enlist, to encourage, and to enable the child to do it. Fathers and grandfathers are not exempt in this responsibility either. A few years hence, or perchance it may be a few decades, he win return to thank you for that priceless heritage, and the spiritual fruitage in his life will be your reward.

The great English scholar, *John Ruskin*, was made to memorize the entire 119th Psalm, which has 176 verses. He said his mother made him memorize it, and that he did not think he would ever like that Scripture. In adulthood he wrote, "It is strange that of all the pieces of the Bible which my mother taught me, that which cost me most to learn, and which was to my child's mind most repulsive—the 119th Psalm—has now become of all the most precious to me in its overflowing and glorious passion of love for the law of God."

N. A. WOYCHUK

The Fruit of Memorizing Scripture

In enrolling to memorize Scripture, you have undertaken about the greatest thing a boy or girl can do. God is able to bless in a special way and to use mightily the person who will spend time to take in what God has to say. Like *President Woodrow Wilson* once said, "The Bible is the Word of life. I beg that you find this out for yourself... You will find the Bible the key to your own heart, your own happiness, and your own duty-"

Take time to enjoy God's word and to memorize it well. Let God speak to you through it and meet your every need.

Here is a story about a boy who memorized Scripture about 160 years ago. His name was Robert. In school he was known as a dunce because it seemed he was too stupid to learn.

If Robert did not learn at school he learned at home. Every morning his father took down the big Bible and read it and prayed with his family. His mother loved the Scriptures, too. So many a day Robert sat with his Bible open committing to memory portions from its pages. Probably he often longed to shut the book and run outside to join with his companions in their games. But his mother held him to the task. At 12 years of age he could recite the whole of Psalm 119. That is the longest chapter in the Bible.

One day the minister from the Presbyterian Church visited them. He had heard that Robert knew Psalm 119 by memory. "I would like to have him repeat it in our church," said he.

The next Sunday this 12 year old boy stood in front of the big congregation and recited perfectly the 119th Psalm. Believe it or not, from the time that Robert started to memorize Scripture he improved in his school work.

Better still, while a boy he received into his heart Christ Jesus the Lord. He wrote out a pledge thus: "Jesus, I have given myself to Thy service. I learn from Thy Word that it is Thy holy pleasure that the gospel shall be preached to all nations. I desire to go where I am most needed."

In the year 1807 he sailed for China, the very first Protestant missionary. In a letter to a friend he told how it was the memorizing of Scripture when a boy that influenced him to become a missionary.

He not only learned to speak their language like a Chinese person after a time, but he translated the Bible into that language, and wrote an English-Chinese dictionary in six very large volumes.

Today, that boy who was known as a dunce is remembered as *Robert Morrison* who did a work for China that has probably never been equalled. And it all started with the memorization of Scripture!

Oh, blessed, blessed Bible,
God's messenger of love
For lifting needy children
To higher planes above.

'Tis a light unto my pathway,
'Tis old, yet ever new;
I'm acquainted with the Author,
And I know the Book is true.

God's Word Comes From God

God used about 40 writers, separated by hundreds of miles, in giving us the Bible.

How wonderful that 40 writers, over a period of 1,500 years, should write a Book that agrees together as one! It is really a Miracle Book. The reason for that is this: *God did all the thinking in the Bible.* The thoughts in the Bible are all God's thoughts. The Scriptures in our assignment tell us that the prophets wrote as they were "moved," "inspired," or "carried along" by the Holy Spirit of God.

Freddy was eight years old. There was no Bible in his home. He came to Sunday School for the first time. "What is the Bible?" he said to the teacher. Teacher: "The Word of God."

Freddy: "Of what use is it?" Teacher: "It tells us of God's love and how we may become His children."

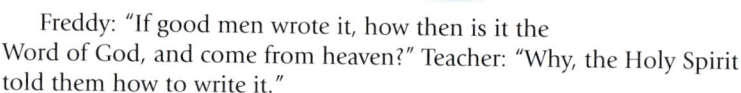

Freddy: "Where did the Bible come from?" Teacher: "From heaven, really." Freddy: "Was it written in heaven?" Teacher: "No, the prophets and good men of God wrote it."

Freddy: "If good men wrote it, how then is it the Word of God, and come from heaven?" Teacher: "Why, the Holy Spirit told them how to write it."

Freddy: "Did they see the Holy Spirit, and did He speak to them?" Teacher: "No, but He made them think it. King David was one man whom the Spirit used in writing the Bible, and here is how David explains it, 'The Spirit of the Lord spoke by me, and His word was on my tongue' (2 Sam. 23:2)."

EXPLANATION OF WORDS
lay up—store away, treasure
proclaimed—made it known
inspiration of God—God-breathed, altogether from the Lord
prophecy—the words of the Bible
moved—borne along, just like a ship carries a person to his destination

ASSIGNMENT 1
God's Word Comes From God

Job 22:22

Receive, please,
instruction from His mouth,
and lay up His words in your heart.

Psalm 68:11

The Lord gave the word;
great was the company of those
who proclaimed it.

2 Timothy 3:16

All Scripture is given by inspiration of God.

2 Peter 1:21

For prophecy never came
by the will of man,
but holy men of God spoke
as they were moved by
the Holy Spirit.

God's Word Speaks For God

The Bible is the greatest Book in all the world because it is God's Word. It is full of love and power like no other book, because it is full of God.

Kristi and Matt were talking about the Bible. Kristi: "What do you think of the Bible?" Matt: "It is the Word of God."

Kristi: "Is there anything written there that you don't understand?" Matt: "Yes, a great deal."

Kristi: "What do you do with those things that you do not understand?" Matt: "I just think that God is wiser than I am. I pray also that He will please let me know and understand all that He wishes to say to me today."

The Bible, or parts of it, has now been translated into some 2,000 languages. It is estimated that there are over 300,100,000 Bibles in the world. If placed side to side, they would make a line 18,000 miles long.

EXPLANATION OF WORDS
saints—believers, those who have trusted the Lord
fear of the LORD—reverence, deep respect for the Lord
wisdom—good judgment

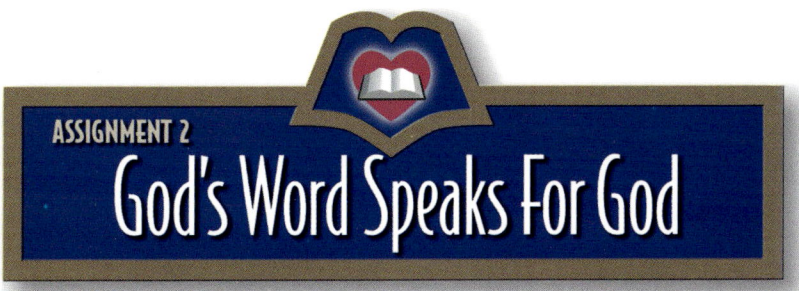

ASSIGNMENT 2
God's Word Speaks For God

Psalm 85:8

I will hear what God the LORD will speak,
for He will speak peace to His people,
and to His saints.

Proverbs 2:1, 5, 6

My son, if you receive my words,
and treasure my commands within you.

Then you will understand the fear of the LORD,
and find the knowledge of God.

For the LORD gives wisdom;
from His mouth
come knowledge and understanding.

God's Word Is Pure

The Word of God is always right, and true and pure. In it we find help and light and comfort. It causes us to love the Lord, and to love other people.

Robert Moffat taught the Word of God to people in Africa. Among these Africans was an old Chief who had a very keen hunting dog. One day the Chief came to Mr. Moffat in great distress and said, "My dog has eaten your New Testament."

"That is too bad," replied the missionary, "but I don't think it will harm your dog, for he is able to eat big bones, and a little book will not make him sick."

"Oh, it's not that," said the Chief. "But your Book is so full of love and gentleness, I'm afraid my dog will never be good for hunting again."

The Bread of Life will feed the soul–
Will make both heart and spirit whole.
The Bread of Life will keep us sweet,
And help us stand when we are beat.
The Bread of Life will make us strong;
Will give us gladness all day long.
The Bread of Life will keep us pure;
Will guard our souls 'gainst sinful lure.

EXPLANATION OF WORDS
tried—tested
statutes—written words, decisions
commandment—instruction, teaching

ASSIGNMENT 3

God's Word Is Pure

Psalm 12:6

The words of the LORD are pure words,
like silver tried in a furnace of earth,
purified seven times.

Psalm 19:8

The statutes of the LORD are right,
rejoicing the heart;
the commandment of the LORD is pure,
enlightening the eyes.

Psalm 119:140

Your word is very pure;
therefore your servant loves it.

Proverbs 30:5

Every word of God is pure;
He is a shield
to those who put their trust in Him.

God's Word Is Sure

God tells us that His Word is true and that it will stand forever.

Through the years, the Bible has had many enemies. At one time in Austria, a law was passed that every Bible in the hands of the people should be burned. Men were sent from door to door to search for Bibles. People who loved their Bibles began to think of ways to hide them.

Mrs. Schebolt had a large family Bible. One day she saw the men coming to her door. She had prepared a great batch of dough to bake bread. Quickly she wrapped her precious Bible and put it in the dough. With this she filled her largest bread-tin. Into the oven it went and baked while the enemies searched the house.

After the men left, she took it out of the loaf, and to her delight, found it unhurt. The Bible is now over 150 years old. It is the property of Mrs. Schebolt's grandson who lives near Maumee City, Ohio.

> *Trust the Word of God,*
> *His promises are sure;*
> *'Tis stable as His mighty throne*
> *And ever shall endure.*

EXPLANATION OF WORDS
settled—fixed, certain
righteous judgments—right decisions
stands—remains unchanged and immovable

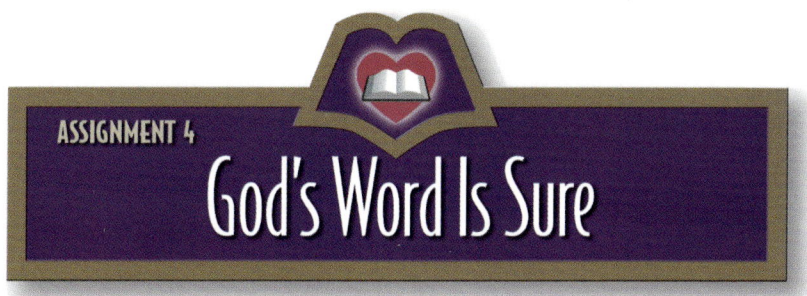

ASSIGNMENT 4
God's Word Is Sure

Psalm 119:89
Forever, O LORD,
Your word is settled in heaven.

Psalm 119:160
The entirety of Your word is truth,
and every one of Your righteous judgments
endures forever.

Isaiah 40:8
The grass withers,
the flower fades,
but the word of our God stands forever.

Matthew 24:35
Heaven and earth will pass away,
but My words will by no means pass away.

His Word Gives Me Light

Just as the sun is the light for this earth, so God's Word is the light for our life and walk with God. It shows us eternal life.

A missionary in Africa saw a native coming toward her, leading a goat. He put down his spear, tied up the goat, and then said, "White lady, has God's Book arrived in our country?" "Are you interested in God's Book?" she inquired.

"Yes," replied the native, "My son brought me these pieces of paper, and has been teaching me the words, 'God so loved the world, that He gave His only begotten Son.' I heard that God's Book had arrived, and I have walked for five days, and brought this goat to buy God's Book."

She then showed him a copy of the Bible, and found the place where the words were printed. "Give me that Book," he said, "and you can keep this goat."

Then he walked up and down before her, pressing the Book to his heart, saying, "God's Book! He has given us light! He has spoken to us in our own language!" Then he returned to his own village with God's Book to give them the light of the gospel.

EXPLANATION OF WORDS
simple—a humble person who does not think himself too smart to learn from God
to heed—to pay attention

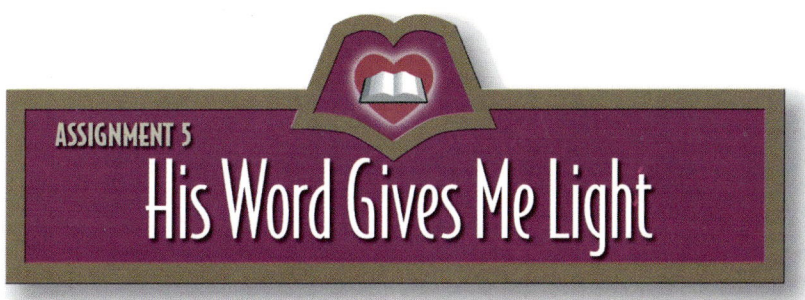

ASSIGNMENT 5
His Word Gives Me Light

Psalm 119:18

Open my eyes,
that I may see wondrous things
from Your law.

Psalm 119:105

Your word is a lamp to my feet
and a light to my path.

Psalm 119:130

The entrance of Your words gives light;
it gives understanding to the simple.

2 Peter 1:19

And so we have the prophetic word confirmed,
which you do well to heed
as a light that shines in a dark place.

His Word Keeps Me Right

God's Word in your heart and mind will keep you from sin, and give you joy.

Some years ago, two little boys were left all alone in London when their parents died. The only friend they had in the world was an uncle. He lived in Liverpool, 200 miles away. So they set off walking to Liverpool to find their uncle.

After walking many, weary miles, they decided to stop for the night in a little town. With their little bundles in their hands, they went to a tourist house. When they were asked to pay, they said they had no money. The manager saw that one of them had, in his coat pocket, a neatly-bound Bible. He offered to buy it for about one dollar.

"No," said the pale-faced boy, as big tears started in his eyes, "We'll starve before we sell the Bible." The man was surprised. He offered them more money again and again, but, each time, they clung to that precious book. "No," they said. "It has been our help all the way from London. Often when tired, or when tempted to do wrong, we have sat down by the roadside, and read in our Bible, and it has seemed like drink and food to us."

"But," said the man, "suppose, when you get to Liverpool, your uncle refuses to help you; what will you do then" "We'll trust that to God," said the younger of the two boys; "for in this book"—laying his hand on the Bible, —"it says, 'When my father and my mother forsake me, then the Lord will take me up!'"

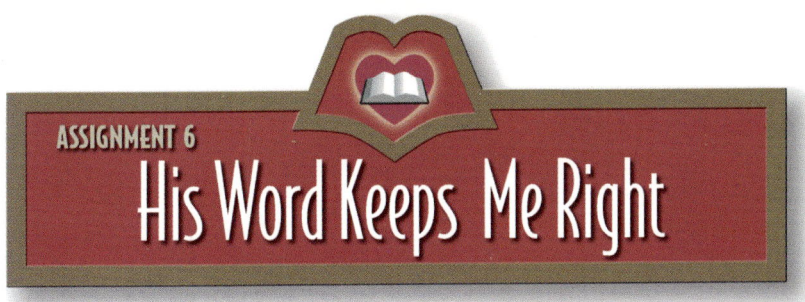

ASSIGNMENT 6

His Word Keeps Me Right

Psalm 37:31
The law of his God is in his heart;
none of his steps shall slide.

Psalm 119:9
How can a young man cleanse his way?
By taking heed according to Your word.

Psalm 119:11
Your word I have hidden in my heart,
that I might not sin against You.

Matthew 22:29
Jesus answered and said to them,
"You are mistaken,
not knowing the Scriptures
nor the power of God."

His Word Is My Delight

It is good to read about people like David and Jeremiah who really loved the Word of God, and enjoyed it more than everything else. There are boys and girls like that too.

Over 400 years ago, there lived a young girl in England whose name was *Lady Jane Grey*. She was a princess, and had everything you could imagine. At 16 years of age she became Queen of England. But she was Queen for only 9 days. Her enemies rose up against her and cruelly beheaded her in the Tower of London.

While Lady Jane was growing up as a princess she loved the Word of God very, very much. She used to read it, meditate upon it and memorize it much of the time. When her parents and friends were out riding and hunting, she would stay at home and enjoy her Bible rather than join them in their amusements.

One day, a friend asked her why she did this. She laid her hand on her Bible, near her, and said, "All other pleasures are only shadows compared to those I find in reading this blessed Book."

EXPLANATION OF WORDS
hosts—great numbers of people

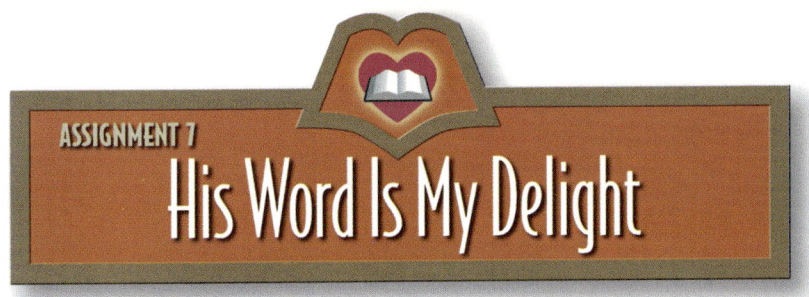

ASSIGNMENT 7
His Word Is My Delight

Psalm 119:16
I will delight myself in Your statutes;
I will not forget Your word.

Psalm 119:47
And I will delight myself in Your commandments,
which I love.

Psalm 119:103
How sweet are Your words to my taste,
sweeter than honey to my mouth!

Jeremiah 15:16
Your words were found,
and I ate them,
and Your word was to me
the joy and rejoicing of my heart;
for I am called by Your name,
O LORD God of hosts.

His Word Is My Defense

Eleanor gave her teacher a paper with this writing on it: "The Bible is a loaf, every chapter is a slice, and every verse a bite."

If I should count the slices
Of bread you eat each day,
And then compare the chapters
Of the Word you stow away;
I wonder just how it would be
When the difference we'd see.

When Mr. Lincoln was a baby, his mother said that she would rather have him learn to read and to enjoy the Bible than to have him own a farm.

As he grew up, he did enjoy and use the Word of God. His very language and speeches became more and more like that of the Bible. In one of his speeches he said, "I believe the Bible is the best gift God has given to man. All the good from the Savior of the world is communicated to us through this Book."

During the Civil War in our country, Mr. Lincoln was president. One night a guest at the White House was not sleeping well. He noticed a light very early in the room next to him. He tiptoed to the door, and saw President Lincoln kneeling at his bedside with the open Bible before him. He was letting God talk to him and instruct him out of His Word.

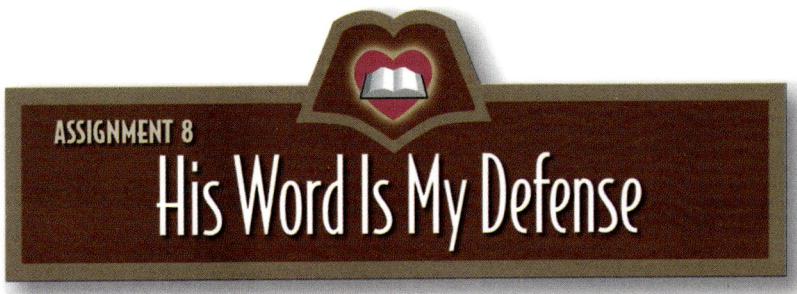

ASSIGNMENT 8
His Word Is My Defense

Psalm 18:30
As for God, His way is perfect;
the word of the LORD is proven;
He is a shield to all who trust in Him.

Matthew 4:4
But He answered and said,
"It is written,
'Man shall not live by bread alone,
but by every word that proceeds
from the mouth of God.'"

Ephesians 6:17
And take the helmet of salvation,
and the sword of the Spirit,
which is the word of God.

Hebrew 4:12
For the word of God is living and powerful,
and sharper than any two-edged sword.

It Is The Seed Of God

When good seed is planted in the ground, it brings a good harvest. God's Word is the seed which God plants in our hearts. Listen to it. Take it seriously. Believe the message, and become "born again." This seed also helps us to become better Christians each day.

John Ruskin was a very great writer and artist. He loved God's Word. He said, "All that I have taught of art, everything that I have written, every greatness that has been in any thought of mine, whatever I have done in my life, has simply been due to the fact that when I was a child, my mother daily read with me a part of the Bible, and daily made me learn a part of it by heart."

EXPLANATION OF WORDS
sheaves—grain tied into bundles
parable—a story that teaches a lesson
corruptible seed—something that can decay or become rotten
incorruptible—that which cannot decay or spoil
abides—remains, lasts

ASSIGNMENT 9
It Is The Seed Of God

Psalm 126:6

He who continually goes forth weeping,
bearing seed for sowing,
shall doubtless come again with rejoicing,
bringing his sheaves with him.

Matthew 13:23

But he who received seed on the good ground
is he who hears the word and understands it,
who indeed bears fruit.

Luke 8:11

Now the parable is this:
The seed is the word of God.

1 Peter 1:23

Having been born again,
not of corruptible seed but incorruptible,
through the word of God
which lives and abides forever.

It Is The Strength Of Prayer

Listen while the Bible talks:

"I am the Bible. I am God's wonderful library. I make known to everybody the Lord Jesus Christ, who is the Truth.

"To the one who sits in darkness, I am glorious light. To him who has lost his way, I am a safe guide.

"To those who carry heavy burdens, I am sweet rest. To the discouraged, I whisper words of good cheer. To those who are hurt by sin, I offer salvation and healing.

"I am God's Word. God speaks through me. Use me."

> *This Book will keep you from sin or sin will keep you from this Book*

A dear old lady, Mrs. FitzGerald, of Newark, N. J., is 90 years of age. She has read the Bible through ninety times. "When I take this Book in my hand," she said, "I know it to be the Word of God. I read it as a miner seeks for gold. Each time I read it, I find something new and precious. It always helps me in prayer."

She has read it in Spanish, German, and French, as well as in English. Asked what her favorite passage is, she said slowly:

"If you abide in Me, and My words abide in you, you will ask what you desire, and it shall be done for you." (John 15:7)

EXPLANATION OF WORDS
admonishing—warning, counseling, guiding
grace—gratitude, thankfulness

ASSIGNMENT 10
It Is The Strength Of Prayer

Psalm 119:171
My lips shall utter praise,
for You teach me Your statutes.

Psalm 130:5
I wait for the LORD,
my soul waits,
and in His word I do hope.

John 15:7
If you abide in Me,
and My words abide in you,
you will ask what you desire,
and it shall be done for you.

Colossians 3:16
Let the word of Christ
dwell in you richly in all wisdom,
teaching and admonishing one another
in psalms and hymns and spiritual songs,
singing with grace in your hearts to the Lord.

It Is The Source Of Faith

The artist uses the brush in painting a picture. The carpenter uses the hammer in driving a nail. The laundress uses water in washing clothes. But God uses the Bible in saving a soul. God's Word gives you something to lay hold of when you come to God. You believe His Word. You come to Him. That is faith.

> *What may be on the morrow*
> *Our foresight cannot see;*
> *But be it joy or sorrow,*
> *We know it comes from Thee.*
> *And nothing can take from us,*
> *Where'er our steps may move,*
> *The staff of Thy sure promise,*
> *The shield of Thy true love.*
>   *—Burns*

Many years ago, an old Scottish laboring man lay dying. The neighbors asked him if they could do anything for him. He said, yes; there was a wee laddie who lived up the hill side, and he would be glad if they would get the lad. They brought the little four-year old chap, and set him at the bedside of the dying man. The boy repeated the 23rd Psalm, and then sang it to him while the old man died listening to the words and the music.

That little lad, who strengthened an old man's faith, became later the great missionary to the people in the New Hebrides. His name was Dr. John G. Paton.

EXPLANATION OF WORDS
assuredly—truly, truthfully
come into judgment—be pronounced guilty
commend you to God—place you in God's hand

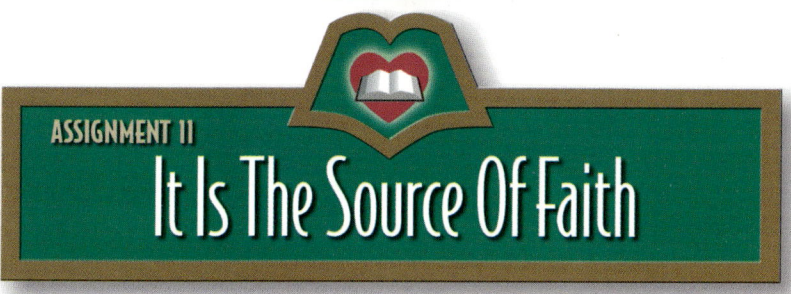

ASSIGNMENT 11

It Is The Source Of Faith

John 5:24
Most assuredly, I say to you,
he who hears My word
and believes in Him who sent Me
has everlasting life,
and shall not come into judgment,
but has passed from death into life.

Acts 20:32
So now, brethren,
I commend you to God
and to the word of His grace,
which is able to build you up.

Romans 10:17
So then faith comes by hearing,
and hearing by the word of God.

1 Peter 2:2
As newborn babes,
desire the pure milk of the word,
that you may grow thereby.

It Is The Secret Of Life

There lived in St. Louis, Mo., a Scotch family, where the old grandmother loved her Bible and studied it daily. The family had to move to another city. They wished to carry with them as little as possible, and got rid of furniture and many personal things.

Grandmother looked at her old Bible. It was so large, worn out, and seemed quite useless. She had good ones to take along. They were burning a lot of rubbish. She took the Bible, and as she approached the fire, she clasped it in her arms, and said, "Never, never can I burn God's Word . . . I shall take it into the garden and bury it as I would the precious body of one I loved." And that's exactly what she did.

Another family moved into the place. They were well-to-do, but cared nothing for either the church or the Bible. They did not even have a Bible in the family. Several months later they were digging in the garden preparing to plant lettuce. The spade struck an object, which they soon discovered was an old Bible.

The grandmother in this family stood by and watched it curiously. Quite excited, she said to the others as she picked up the wet Bible, *"Children, we have no Bible; this has been sent us from the Lord."* She dried it out carefully, and began reading it chapter after chapter. She truly searched the Scriptures, and found that they did speak of the Savior. Soon the Word of God made her "wise unto salvation," and she was converted. Later, all the other members of the family also trusted Christ, and began serving Him together in the church as a family. Truly this Bible was sent to them from the Lord.

EXPLANATION OF WORDS
converting—changing
testify of—tell about
faith—trust, confidence, believing

ASSIGNMENT 12

It Is The Secret Of Life

Psalm 19:7

The law of the LORD is perfect,
converting the soul;
the testimony of the LORD is sure,
making wise the simple.

John 5:39

You search the Scriptures,
for in them you think you have eternal life;
and these are they which testify of Me.

John 8:32

And you shall know the truth,
and the truth shall make you free.

2 Timothy 3:15

And that from childhood
you have known the Holy Scriptures,
which are able to make you wise for salvation
through faith which is in Christ Jesus.

What Is The Bible Like?

THE BIBLE IS LIKE A HOUSE.

It is a tiny house without chimneys or windows. The door is very small, and scores of busy little creatures go in and out all day making a buzzing noise.

What is this house?

Quite right — a Beehive.

The Bible is like a beehive, full of sweetness. There is no sweetness like Bible sweetness. The Psalmist David thought so. Listen to him: "How sweet are Your words to my taste, sweeter than honey to my mouth!" (Psalm 119:103).

THE BIBLE IS LIKE A HOUSE.

It is a good-sized house on the country road. Downstairs are the sitting-rooms and dining-room, and upstairs the bedrooms. People come to stay there for a few days or more and then go home.

What is this house?

Quite right — an Inn.

The Bible is like an inn, full of refreshment. David thought so. Listen to him: "I opened my mouth and panted, for I longed (was hungry) for Your commandments" (Psalm 119:131).

The Bible is like a house.

It is a big and substantial house in a busy street in town and city. Inside are customers at a counter. (No, it is not a shop). On the counter is a lot of money.

What is this house?

Quite right — a Bank.

The Bible is like a bank full of riches. There are no riches like Bible riches. The Psalmist thought so. Listen to him: "The law of Your mouth is better to me than thousands of coins of gold and silver" (Psalm 119:72).

THE BIBLE IS LIKE A HOUSE.

It is very, very tall, and at the top some people live whose work is of first-class importance. It stands, not on the land, but out at sea.

What is this house?

Quite right — a Lighthouse.

The Bible is like a lighthouse full of light. There is no light like Bible light. The Psalmist thought so. Listen to him: "Your word is a lamp to my feet and a light to my path" (Psalm 119:105).

THE BIBLE IS LIKE A HOUSE.

It is very big, and very noisy. Many machines and lights depend on it.

What is this house?

Quite right — an Electric Power-House.

The Bible is like an electric power-house full of power. There is no power like Bible power. Listen to the Psalmist David: "Strengthen me according to Your word" (Psalm 119:28).

Go over these five houses— **B**eehive... **I**nn... **B**ank... **L**ighthouse... **E**lectric Power-House... Their initials spell **BIBLE**.

Let us thank God for the Bible, as we memorize it and read it prayerfully every day—yes, *every* day.

May the Lord help us to find in it the sweetness, the refreshment, the riches, the light, and the power needed for our spiritual growth each day.

Adapted from G. R. H. Wood

Holy Bible, Book Divine

Holy Bible, book divine,
Precious treasure, thou art mine;
Mine to tell me whence I came;
Mine to teach me what I am.

Mine to chide me when I rove;
Mine to show me a Savior's love;
Mine thou art to guide and guard;
Mine to punish or reward.

Mine to tell of joys to come,
And the rebel sinner's doom;
0 thou holy book, divine,
Precious treasure, thou art mine.

—John Burton

To My Pocket-Bible

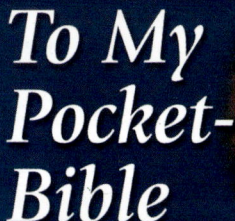

Companion of my walks,
I like thee well;
Far sweeter are thy talks
Than tongue can tell.

I never am alone
When thou art near;
Thy light reveals the throne,
And casts out fear.

Thou art a healing balm,
A friend indeed;
Thy voice creates a calm
In time of need.

Companion, good and true,
Thou art my life;
Thine arm will bear me through
This vale of strife.

—William Anderson

Index

OLD TESTAMENT

Page

Job
- 22:22 11

Psalm
- 12:6 15
- 18:30 25
- 19:7 33
- 19:8 15
- 37:31 21
- 68:11 11
- 85:8 13
- 119:9 21
- 119:11 21
- 119:16 23
- 119:18 19
- 119:47 23
- 119:89 17

Page

Psalm
- 119:103 23
- 119:105 19
- 119:130 19
- 119:140 15
- 119:160 29
- 119:171 33
- 126:6 27
- 130:5 29

Proverbs
- 2:1,5,6 13
- 30:5 15

Isaiah
- 40:8 17

Jeremiah
- 15:16 23

NEW TESTAMENT

Matthew
- 4:4 25
- 13:23 27
- 22:29 21
- 24:35 17

Luke
- 8:11 27

John
- 5:24 31
- 5:39 33
- 8:32 33
- 15:7 29

Acts
- 20:32 31

Romans
- 10:17 31

Ephesians
- 6:17 25

Colossians
- 3:16 29

2 Timothy
- 3:15 33
- 3:16 11

Hebrews
- 4:12 25

1 Peter
- 1:23 27
- 2:2 31

2 Peter
- 1:19 19
- 1:21 11